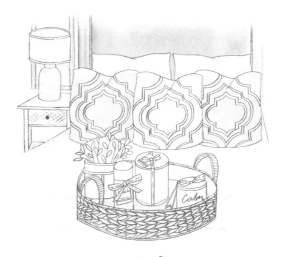

Mrs Hinch

LIFE IN LISTS

MICHAEL JOSEPH

UK | USA | Canada | Ireland | Australia
India | New Zealand | South Africa

Michael Joseph is part of the Penguin Random House group of companies
whose addresses can be found at global.penguinrandomhouse.com

First published 2021
001

Copyright © Mrs Hinch 2021

The moral right of the author has been asserted

Set in Archer and Golden Plains
Designed and typeset by Smith & Gilmour
Creative consultant Joey Morrison
Printed in Germany by GGP Media GmbH, Poessneck

The authorised representative in the EEA is Penguin Random House Ireland,
Morrison Chambers, 32 Nassau Street, Dublin D02 YH68

Illustrations © Lindsey Spinks, except for
pages 180 & 182 © May van Millingen; page 216 © Shutterstock
Quotation on page 91 © Fast Company, a registered
trademark of Mansueto Ventures LLC
Quotation on page 135 © Paulo Coelho
Every effort has been made to trace copyright holders and to obtain their
permission for the use of copyright material. The publisher apologises
for any errors or omissions and would be grateful if notified of any corrections
that should be incorporated in future reprints or editions of this book.

A CIP catalogue record for this book is available from the British Library

ISBN: 978-0-241-55099-1

www.greenpenguin.co.uk

Penguin Random House is committed to a
sustainable future for our business, our readers
and our planet. This book is made from Forest
Stewardship Council® certified paper.

Mrs Hinch

LIFE IN LISTS

WASH UP

MICHAEL JOSEPH

PENGUIN
Est. 1935

Hi Guys!

Sophie here!

Welcome to my new notebook, *Life in Lists*.

If I were to explain *Life in Lists* to you, I like to see it as *The Little Book of Lists*' sidekick. I've received so many amazing messages about how helpful you've found *The Little Book of Lists* and how much you love using it to organise your day. Many of you have said, 'It would be just perfect if there was a list for this… and what about a list for that…', so that is exactly how *Life in Lists* came to be.

What You'll Find Inside:

With this notebook, I wanted to achieve a basic structure so it's there if you need it, but also enough room for these lists to be as flexible and as much your own as you want them to be.

    In the hinching section there are Hinch Lists, Monthly Hinch Lists, Seasonal Hinch Lists, Tadaas and Fresh'n Up Fridays. As you know, I keep on top of our home by doing little and often because that's what has always worked best for me. I've never really enjoyed too much of a rigid cleaning routine because I don't think we should be putting any unnecessary pressure on ourselves (which is why Tadaas will always be one of my faves). But I do notice there are specific tasks I tend to do at similar times, so I've included more specific examples, as some of you have said you'd really love to get more of an idea of what I do when, and how often. Although please remember, I'm slightly obsessed with cleaning, tidying and organising, so you absolutely don't need to do as much as me! You just need to work out what works best for you, your little family and your home.

My Hinch List will always be at the heart of everything I do. I love using it to go around the house and make a note of those bits that need doing as I see them, so I won't forget. You will also notice in this book that there aren't any labels, so you have the whole double page to make your own. You'll see that I like to organise mine room by room, but I almost always have a 'Bits and Bobs' section. I also love a Hinch Haul section to write down anything we run out of as and when it happens, so I can remember to pick those things up from the shop.

In this notebook I've also added some Monthly and Seasonal Hinch Lists. Once I've written down what I need to get done for the relevant month and season, I like to spread those tasks across several main Hinch lists, to make them more manageable. And don't worry guys if you don't get to them all! They aren't going anywhere! I just find that if I keep on top of things in this way, those little things every so often are more achievable for me. But it's all about whatever works for you.

I wanted you to have space to plan things like your big spring cleans, and the big sort-out we all inevitably end up doing before the holiday season. That's what I love most about this book. The fact that you can use it for so many different things, and it just works!

We've still got our all-important Tadaas and Fresh'n Up Fridays. I just couldn't bring out a notebook without those in it because I love and rely on them so much! Tadaas are so perfect for those days when a to-do just seems too much. I find myself using them more and more to write down what I've achieved on the days I'm feeling a bit overwhelmed. I love that you've managed to make them work for you too!

And last but not least, of course we still have our Fresh'n Up Fridays. I love to pick at least three rooms in the house and three things that need doing in each of those rooms to give our home a little bit of a freshen up, ready for the weekend.

In the next part of the book, let me introduce you to our new Me Time Lists, Gratitude Lists and Make Your Dreams Come True pages. I noticed that some of you have also been using your Tadaas to plan your self-care, which I love. So there's a space for you to do that now. It's so important that we remember to look after ourselves as well as we look after everyone else that we love. We all get so busy that it feels easier to put taking care of others in front of taking care of us. But don't forget, you matter too! We often say that we can't find the time for self-care with everything else going on, but I'd really like to encourage you to try and do that with these pages. It's amazing what you can do to relax that doesn't take very much time at all. I've included some examples if you're finding it tricky to think of ideas.

I find the more time I practise focusing on and appreciating the things I have in life to be grateful for, the more I start to automatically notice those things without even trying. It's so important to put things into perspective. It makes us less likely to get pulled down when life doesn't always go to plan, because we've got so many amazing things to be thankful for. That's why this book includes a Gratitude section, so that we can reflect back on each day with three things that made us smile the most.

We've also got Make Your Dreams Come True pages in *Life in Lists*. I read once that you are so much more likely to achieve something if you make yourself a plan: write it down and visualise it, and that's really stuck with me. I think people can sometimes be intimidated by the idea of setting goals, but I see them as a way of making my dreams come true. Those things in life I'd absolutely love to achieve. No matter how little or big they are, if you break them down into manageable pieces and set out how you're going to make them happen, you'll get on and do it. I truly believe that.

In the last section of the book there are some list and note pages for you to use for absolutely everything else. There are a variety of layouts and I hope you'll find these really useful. A lot of you may also notice the familiar little drawings throughout that you can colour in, if you like doing that sort of thing.

I really hope you guys enjoy *Life in Lists* as much as I've enjoyed putting it together for you. It really is a one-stop shop, and I hope you find it as relaxing as you do organisational. And please don't forget to tag me in your #hinchlist. I really love seeing how you all use yours! I get so many useful ideas from them! That's one of the things that I love most about this community we've all built. I could never say it enough. Thank you for supporting me and my little family as much as you always do. You're such a big part of our lives!

Lots of Love Always,
Soph xx

HINCH LISTS

Date: _Monday 10th_

My Hinch List

KITCHEN

- Oven filter, liners, trays ☑
- Organise food cupboards ☑
- Wipe cupboard shelves ☑
- Deep clean floor ☐
- Sort veg rack ☐
- Toaster ☑
- Washing machine clean ☐
- Tidy under-sink cupboard ☐

BATHROOM

- Bath ☐
- Shower screen ☐
- Sink ☑
- Wipe & pine toilet ☑
- Windows ☐
- Towel rail ☐
- Drawers ☐
- Mop floor ☐

LOUNGE

- Restock tealights ☐
- Wash curtains ☐
- Wash throws ☑
- Wipe rads ☐
- Clean mirrors ☑
- Dave & Sheen ☐
- Vacuum sofa ☐
- Dust blinds ☐

GARDEN

- Clean outside windows ☐
- Jet wash patio ☑
- Clean rattan furniture ☐
- Wash outside cushion covers ☑
- Check & replace solars ☑
- Fertilise beds ☐
- Clean pergola mirror ☑
- Tidy Ron's Wendy house ☐

A typical example of my Hinch List!

NURSERY

- Tidy clothes away ✓
- Paint touch-ups ☐
- Restock caddy ✓
- Refill bottles ✓
- Sanitise nappy bin ☐
- Wash toy bears ☐
- Clean windowsill ☐
- Dust blinds ☐

BITS AND BOBS

- Sort wax melts ☐
- Clean car seats ✓
- Febreze fabrics ☐
- Sort stairs basket ✓
- Vacuum mattresses ☐
- Dust hunt ☐
- Clean indoor plants ☐
- Charity shop run ☐

GARAGE

- Sort and clean fridge ☐
- Vacuum & mop floor ☐
- TerraCycle boxes ✓
- Sort post ✓
- Sort deliveries ✓
- Dryer filter ☐
- Restock cleaning trolley ☐
- Check Kallax boxes ☐

HINCH HAUL

- Ham ☐
- Chicken ☐
- Eggs ☐
- Milk ☐
- Spinach ☐
- Mince ☐
- Ketchup ☐
- Bleach ☐

11

Date: January 2024.

My Hinch List

Kitchen.
- Clean cupboards ☐
- clean Draws ☐
- clean Fridge. ☑
- clean Washing machine. ☐
- clean Tumble Dryer. ☐
- clean cooker. Deepclean ☑
- clean Blinds, Rads, ☐
- Wipe walls door + Window ☐
- clean doors ✓

Bathroom.
- Sort out cabinet. ☑
- Sort out cupboard. ☑
- deep clean Toilet. ☑
- deep clean shower. ☐
- Wipe walls + Blinds ☐
- Clean doors ☑
- ☐
- ☐

2 Hallways
- wipe walls down ☐
- wipe skirting boards ☑
- clean lights. ☐
- clean + sort cupboard ☑
- cleans doors ☑
- ☐
- ☐
- ☐

Dinning-Room.
- Clean drinks cabinet out ☑
- clean glasses. ☑
- polish table + chairs ☑
- clean patio door. ☐
- vac curtains ☐
- clean lights ☐
- wipe walls + Radiators ☑
- clean patio windows ☑

12

Bedroom

- Clean + sort out my wardrobe ✓
- Clean + sort out bills wardrobe ✓
- Sort out all shoes. ✓
- Clean window + lights ☐
- Clean + declutter draws. ✓
- Wipe walls ☐
- Deep clean bed + mattress ✓
- Vac curtains. ☐

Spare Bedroom.

- Wipe walls down + rads. ☐
- Clean windows ☐
- Declutter + clean my wardrobe ✓
- Declutter + clean bills wardrobe ✓
- Clean + declutter all draws ✓
- ☐
- ☐
- ☐

- ☐
- ☐
- ☐
- ☐
- ☐
- ☐
- ☐
- ☐

- ☐
- ☐
- ☐
- ☐
- ☐
- ☐
- ☐
- ☐

Date: ....

My Hinch List

_____

- .... ☐
- .... ☐
- .... ☐
- .... ☐
- .... ☐
- .... ☐
- .... ☐
- .... ☐

_____

- .... ☐
- .... ☐
- .... ☐
- .... ☐
- .... ☐
- .... ☐
- .... ☐
- .... ☐

_____

- .... ☐
- .... ☐
- .... ☐
- .... ☐
- .... ☐
- .... ☐
- .... ☐
- .... ☐

_____

- .... ☐
- .... ☐
- .... ☐
- .... ☐
- .... ☐
- .... ☐
- .... ☐
- .... ☐

I'd love to see your #hinchlist!

Don't forget to tag me on 📷

- _____ ☐
- _____ ☐
- _____ ☐
- _____ ☐
- _____ ☐
- _____ ☐
- _____ ☐
- _____ ☐

- _____ ☐
- _____ ☐
- _____ ☐
- _____ ☐
- _____ ☐
- _____ ☐
- _____ ☐
- _____ ☐

- _____ ☐
- _____ ☐
- _____ ☐
- _____ ☐
- _____ ☐
- _____ ☐
- _____ ☐
- _____ ☐

- _____ ☐
- _____ ☐
- _____ ☐
- _____ ☐
- _____ ☐
- _____ ☐
- _____ ☐
- _____ ☐

My Hinch List

- ☐
- ☐
- ☐
- ☐
- ☐
- ☐
- ☐
- ☐

- ☐
- ☐
- ☐
- ☐
- ☐
- ☐
- ☐
- ☐

- ☐
- ☐
- ☐
- ☐
- ☐
- ☐
- ☐
- ☐

- ☐
- ☐
- ☐
- ☐
- ☐
- ☐
- ☐
- ☐

My Hinch List

_____

_____
- .... ☐
- .... ☐
- .... ☐
- .... ☐
- .... ☐
- .... ☐
- .... ☐
- .... ☐

_____

_____
- .... ☐
- .... ☐
- .... ☐
- .... ☐
- .... ☐
- .... ☐
- .... ☐
- .... ☐

_____

_____
- .... ☐
- .... ☐
- .... ☐
- .... ☐
- .... ☐
- .... ☐
- .... ☐
- .... ☐

_____

_____
- .... ☐
- .... ☐
- .... ☐
- .... ☐
- .... ☐
- .... ☐
- .... ☐
- .... ☐

_____

_____
- .... ☐
- .... ☐
- .... ☐
- .... ☐
- .... ☐
- .... ☐
- .... ☐
- .... ☐

_____

_____
- .... ☐
- .... ☐
- .... ☐
- .... ☐
- .... ☐
- .... ☐
- .... ☐
- .... ☐

_____

_____
- .... ☐
- .... ☐
- .... ☐
- .... ☐
- .... ☐
- .... ☐
- .... ☐
- .... ☐

_____

_____
- .... ☐
- .... ☐
- .... ☐
- .... ☐
- .... ☐
- .... ☐
- .... ☐
- .... ☐

Date: ....

My Hinch List

- ☐
- ☐
- ☐
- ☐
- ☐
- ☐
- ☐
- ☐

- ☐
- ☐
- ☐
- ☐
- ☐
- ☐
- ☐
- ☐

- ☐
- ☐
- ☐
- ☐
- ☐
- ☐
- ☐
- ☐

- ☐
- ☐
- ☐
- ☐
- ☐
- ☐
- ☐
- ☐

My Hinch List

- .... ☐
- .... ☐
- .... ☐
- .... ☐
- .... ☐
- .... ☐
- .... ☐
- .... ☐

- .... ☐
- .... ☐
- .... ☐
- .... ☐
- .... ☐
- .... ☐
- .... ☐
- .... ☐

- .... ☐
- .... ☐
- .... ☐
- .... ☐
- .... ☐
- .... ☐
- .... ☐
- .... ☐

- .... ☐
- .... ☐
- .... ☐
- .... ☐
- .... ☐
- .... ☐
- .... ☐
- .... ☐

I'd love to see your #hinchlist!

Don't forget to tag me on 📷

_____

_____

- ⬜
- ⬜
- ⬜
- ⬜
- ⬜
- ⬜
- ⬜
- ⬜

_____

_____

- ⬜
- ⬜
- ⬜
- ⬜
- ⬜
- ⬜
- ⬜
- ⬜

_____

_____

- ⬜
- ⬜
- ⬜
- ⬜
- ⬜
- ⬜
- ⬜
- ⬜

_____

_____

- ⬜
- ⬜
- ⬜
- ⬜
- ⬜
- ⬜
- ⬜
- ⬜

Date: ....

My Hinch List

_____

_____

- .... ☐
- .... ☐
- .... ☐
- .... ☐
- .... ☐
- .... ☐
- .... ☐
- .... ☐

_____

_____

- .... ☐
- .... ☐
- .... ☐
- .... ☐
- .... ☐
- .... ☐
- .... ☐
- .... ☐

_____

- .... ☐
- .... ☐
- .... ☐
- .... ☐
- .... ☐
- .... ☐
- .... ☐
- .... ☐

_____

- .... ☐
- .... ☐
- .... ☐
- .... ☐
- .... ☐
- .... ☐
- .... ☐
- .... ☐

_____

_____
- .... ☐
- .... ☐
- .... ☐
- .... ☐
- .... ☐
- .... ☐
- .... ☐
- .... ☐

_____
- .... ☐
- .... ☐
- .... ☐
- .... ☐
- .... ☐
- .... ☐
- .... ☐
- .... ☐

_____

_____
- .... ☐
- .... ☐
- .... ☐
- .... ☐
- .... ☐
- .... ☐
- .... ☐
- .... ☐

_____
- .... ☐
- .... ☐
- .... ☐
- .... ☐
- .... ☐
- .... ☐
- .... ☐
- .... ☐

Date: ....

My Hinch List

_____

- .... ☐
- .... ☐
- .... ☐
- .... ☐
- .... ☐
- .... ☐
- .... ☐
- .... ☐

_____

- .... ☐
- .... ☐
- .... ☐
- .... ☐
- .... ☐
- .... ☐
- .... ☐
- .... ☐

_____

- .... ☐
- .... ☐
- .... ☐
- .... ☐
- .... ☐
- .... ☐
- .... ☐
- .... ☐

_____

- .... ☐
- .... ☐
- .... ☐
- .... ☐
- .... ☐
- .... ☐
- .... ☐
- .... ☐

_____

- .... ☐
- .... ☐
- .... ☐
- .... ☐
- .... ☐
- .... ☐
- .... ☐
- .... ☐

_____

- .... ☐
- .... ☐
- .... ☐
- .... ☐
- .... ☐
- .... ☐
- .... ☐
- .... ☐

_____

- .... ☐
- .... ☐
- .... ☐
- .... ☐
- .... ☐
- .... ☐
- .... ☐
- .... ☐

_____

- .... ☐
- .... ☐
- .... ☐
- .... ☐
- .... ☐
- .... ☐
- .... ☐
- .... ☐

Date: ....

My Hinch List

- ☐
- ☐
- ☐
- ☐
- ☐
- ☐
- ☐
- ☐

- ☐
- ☐
- ☐
- ☐
- ☐
- ☐
- ☐
- ☐

- ☐
- ☐
- ☐
- ☐
- ☐
- ☐
- ☐
- ☐

- ☐
- ☐
- ☐
- ☐
- ☐
- ☐
- ☐
- ☐

_____

_____

- .... ☐
- .... ☐
- .... ☐
- .... ☐
- .... ☐
- .... ☐
- .... ☐
- .... ☐

_____

_____

- .... ☐
- .... ☐
- .... ☐
- .... ☐
- .... ☐
- .... ☐
- .... ☐
- .... ☐

_____

_____

- .... ☐
- .... ☐
- .... ☐
- .... ☐
- .... ☐
- .... ☐
- .... ☐
- .... ☐

_____

_____

- .... ☐
- .... ☐
- .... ☐
- .... ☐
- .... ☐
- .... ☐
- .... ☐
- .... ☐

My Hinch List

_____

- .... ☐
- .... ☐
- .... ☐
- .... ☐
- .... ☐
- .... ☐
- .... ☐
- .... ☐

_____

- .... ☐
- .... ☐
- .... ☐
- .... ☐
- .... ☐
- .... ☐
- .... ☐
- .... ☐

_____

- .... ☐
- .... ☐
- .... ☐
- .... ☐
- .... ☐
- .... ☐
- .... ☐
- .... ☐

_____

- .... ☐
- .... ☐
- .... ☐
- .... ☐
- .... ☐
- .... ☐
- .... ☐
- .... ☐

I'd love to see your #hinchlist!

Don't forget to tag me on 📷

- _____ ☐
- _____ ☐
- _____ ☐
- _____ ☐
- _____ ☐
- _____ ☐
- _____ ☐
- _____ ☐

- _____ ☐
- _____ ☐
- _____ ☐
- _____ ☐
- _____ ☐
- _____ ☐
- _____ ☐
- _____ ☐

- _____ ☐
- _____ ☐
- _____ ☐
- _____ ☐
- _____ ☐
- _____ ☐
- _____ ☐
- _____ ☐

- _____ ☐
- _____ ☐
- _____ ☐
- _____ ☐
- _____ ☐
- _____ ☐
- _____ ☐
- _____ ☐

My Hinch List

- ☐
- ☐
- ☐
- ☐
- ☐
- ☐
- ☐
- ☐

- ☐
- ☐
- ☐
- ☐
- ☐
- ☐
- ☐
- ☐

- ☐
- ☐
- ☐
- ☐
- ☐
- ☐
- ☐
- ☐

- ☐
- ☐
- ☐
- ☐
- ☐
- ☐
- ☐
- ☐

Date: ....

My Hinch List

- ☐
- ☐
- ☐
- ☐
- ☐
- ☐
- ☐
- ☐

- ☐
- ☐
- ☐
- ☐
- ☐
- ☐
- ☐
- ☐

- ☐
- ☐
- ☐
- ☐
- ☐
- ☐
- ☐
- ☐

- ☐
- ☐
- ☐
- ☐
- ☐
- ☐
- ☐
- ☐

_____

- .... ☐
- .... ☐
- .... ☐
- .... ☐
- .... ☐
- .... ☐
- .... ☐
- .... ☐

_____

- .... ☐
- .... ☐
- .... ☐
- .... ☐
- .... ☐
- .... ☐
- .... ☐
- .... ☐

_____

- .... ☐
- .... ☐
- .... ☐
- .... ☐
- .... ☐
- .... ☐
- .... ☐
- .... ☐

_____

- .... ☐
- .... ☐
- .... ☐
- .... ☐
- .... ☐
- .... ☐
- .... ☐
- .... ☐

Date: ....

My Hinch List

_____

- .... ☐
- .... ☐
- .... ☐
- .... ☐
- .... ☐
- .... ☐
- .... ☐
- .... ☐

_____

- .... ☐
- .... ☐
- .... ☐
- .... ☐
- .... ☐
- .... ☐
- .... ☐
- .... ☐

_____

- .... ☐
- .... ☐
- .... ☐
- .... ☐
- .... ☐
- .... ☐
- .... ☐
- .... ☐

_____

- .... ☐
- .... ☐
- .... ☐
- .... ☐
- .... ☐
- .... ☐
- .... ☐
- .... ☐

My Hinch List

- ☐
- ☐
- ☐
- ☐
- ☐
- ☐
- ☐
- ☐

- ☐
- ☐
- ☐
- ☐
- ☐
- ☐
- ☐
- ☐

- ☐
- ☐
- ☐
- ☐
- ☐
- ☐
- ☐
- ☐

- ☐
- ☐
- ☐
- ☐
- ☐
- ☐
- ☐
- ☐

I'd love to see your #hinchlist!

Don't forget to tag me on [Instagram]

- .... ☐
- .... ☐
- .... ☐
- .... ☐
- .... ☐
- .... ☐
- .... ☐
- .... ☐

- .... ☐
- .... ☐
- .... ☐
- .... ☐
- .... ☐
- .... ☐
- .... ☐
- .... ☐

- .... ☐
- .... ☐
- .... ☐
- .... ☐
- .... ☐
- .... ☐
- .... ☐
- .... ☐

- .... ☐
- .... ☐
- .... ☐
- .... ☐
- .... ☐
- .... ☐
- .... ☐
- .... ☐

MONTHLY
HINCH
LISTS

My Monthly Hinch List

MAY

- Washing machine clean ✓
- Dishwasher clean ☐
- Deep clean microwave ☐
- Organise food cupboards ✓
- Wipe cupboard shelves ✓
- Clean cupboard doors ✓
- Clean cutlery drawer ☐
- Oven filters, liners & racks ✓

- Check freezer & wipe ☐
- Wash bin ☐
- Clean mirrors ✓
- Vacuum filters ✓
- Clean blinds/shutters ☐
- Vacuum mattresses ✓
- Wipe radiators ✓
- Move furniture & vacuum rugs ☐

- Wipe TV & electronics ☐
- Vacuum sofa ✓
- Dust lampshades ☐
- Check & treat mould/grouting ☐
- Descale showerheads ☐
- Cobwebs ☐
- Internal doors & handles ☐
- Switches & sockets ☐

- Dust skirting ✓
- Windowsills & tracks ☐
- French doors ☐
- External door tracks ✓
- Outside windows ✓
- Washing line ☐
- Sweep & clean artificial grass ☐
- Garage floor ✓

A typical example of tasks I carry out monthly!

My Monthly Hinch List

FEB

- Clean out wardrobes ☐
- clean drawers ☐
- Clean skirting boards ☐
- Clean Dining room ☐
- Deep clean SPARE room ☐
- Deep clean Bathroom ☐
- Sort B/room cupboard ☐
- Do Grouting in B/room ☑
- Clean kitchen c/boards ☐
- Clean cooker ☐
- Clean washing machine ☐
- Clean T/Dryer ☐
- Clean windows ☐
- All floors STEAM ☐
- Clean all mirrors ☐
- Vac under sofas ☐
- ☐
- ☐

WASH UP

43

My Monthly Hinch List

My Monthly Hinch List

My Monthly Hinch List

My Monthly Hinch List

- [ ]
- [ ]
- [ ]
- [ ]
- [ ]
- [ ]
- [ ]
- [ ]
- [ ]
- [ ]
- [ ]
- [ ]
- [ ]
- [ ]
- [ ]
- [ ]
- [ ]
- [ ]

- [ ]
- [ ]
- [ ]
- [ ]
- [ ]
- [ ]
- [ ]
- [ ]
- [ ]
- [ ]
- [ ]
- [ ]
- [ ]
- [ ]
- [ ]
- [ ]
- [ ]
- [ ]

My Monthly Hinch List

- .... ☐
- .... ☐
- .... ☐
- .... ☐
- .... ☐
- .... ☐
- .... ☐
- .... ☐
- .... ☐
- .... ☐
- .... ☐
- .... ☐
- .... ☐
- .... ☐
- .... ☐
- .... ☐
- .... ☐
- .... ☐

- .... ☐
- .... ☐
- .... ☐
- .... ☐
- .... ☐
- .... ☐
- .... ☐
- .... ☐
- .... ☐
- .... ☐
- .... ☐
- .... ☐
- .... ☐
- .... ☐
- .... ☐
- .... ☐
- .... ☐
- .... ☐

My Monthly Hinch List

- [ ]
- [ ]
- [ ]
- [ ]
- [ ]
- [ ]
- [ ]
- [ ]
- [ ]

- [ ]
- [ ]
- [ ]
- [ ]
- [ ]
- [ ]
- [ ]
- [ ]
- [ ]

- [ ]
- [ ]
- [ ]
- [ ]
- [ ]
- [ ]
- [ ]
- [ ]

- [ ]
- [ ]
- [ ]
- [ ]
- [ ]
- [ ]
- [ ]
- [ ]

My Monthly Hinch List

My Monthly Hinch List

My Monthly Hinch List

My Monthly Hinch List

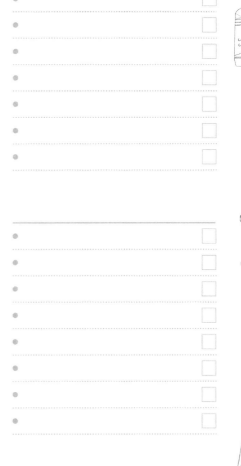

- [ ]
- [ ]
- [ ]
- [ ]
- [ ]
- [ ]
- [ ]
- [ ]

- [ ]
- [ ]
- [ ]
- [ ]
- [ ]
- [ ]
- [ ]
- [ ]

- [ ]
- [ ]
- [ ]
- [ ]
- [ ]
- [ ]
- [ ]

- [ ]
- [ ]
- [ ]
- [ ]
- [ ]
- [ ]
- [ ]

SEASONAL HINCH LISTS

My Seasonal Hinch Lists

- Declutter winter clothes/shoes ☐
- Vacuum pack winter clothes ☐
- Organise summer clothes/shoes ☐
- Wash curtains* ☑
- Bicarb mattress & wash pillows* ☐
- Wash & change winter duvets ☐
- Shampoo sofas, carpet & rugs* ☐
- Change scents (candles, wax ☐
  melts, plug-ins, diffusers etc)

- Clean doormats* ☐
- Clean front & back door* ☐
- Outside lights ☑
- Jet wash patio & front paving ☐
- Clean garden furniture ☑
- Wash outside cushion covers ☑
- Clean garden ornaments ☐
- Check expiries & declutter ☐
  make-up products & skincare

SUMMER

- Organise Narnia & stock check* ☐
- Organise & restock under sink* ☐
- Restock first-aid box ☐
- Clean light shades & fixtures* ☐
- Damp dust skirting* ☐
- Organise stairs Space Tidy ☐
- Sort under-bed storage ☐
- Pick 2 rooms – declutter & ☐
  clean cupboards & drawers*

- Sort other kitchen cupboards* ☐
- Clean behind appliances ☐
- Wipe house plant leaves* ☐
- Paint garden fences/planters ☐
- Deep clean BBQ/grill ☐
- Clean garden toys* ☐
- Jet wash outside bins & shed* ☐
- Sort out garage Kallax unit ☐

My Spring Hinch List

My Summer Hinch List

- _____ ☐
- _____ ☐
- _____ ☐
- _____ ☐
- _____ ☐
- _____ ☐
- _____ ☐
- _____ ☐
- _____ ☐

- _____ ☐
- _____ ☐
- _____ ☐
- _____ ☐
- _____ ☐
- _____ ☐
- _____ ☐
- _____ ☐
- _____ ☐

My Summer Hinch List

My Autumn Hinch List

My Winter Hinch List

- put winter curtains up ☐
- deep clean mattress + bed ☐
- deep clean washing machine ☐
- deep clean Tumbl dryer ☐
- clean kitchen cupboards ☐
- Arrange all food Tins etc ☐
- Deep clean cooker ☐
- cover garden furniture ☐
- ☐

- ☐
- ☐
- ☐
- ☐
- ☐
- ☐
- ☐
- ☐
- ☐

- ☐
- ☐
- ☐
- ☐
- ☐
- ☐
- ☐
- ☐
- ☐

- ☐
- ☐
- ☐
- ☐
- ☐
- ☐
- ☐
- ☐
- ☐

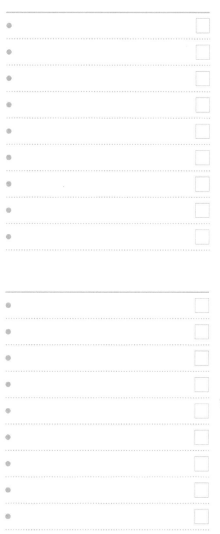

- .... ☐
- .... ☐
- .... ☐
- .... ☐
- .... ☐
- .... ☐
- .... ☐
- .... ☐
- .... ☐

- .... ☐
- .... ☐
- .... ☐
- .... ☐
- .... ☐
- .... ☐
- .... ☐
- .... ☐
- .... ☐

- .... ☐
- .... ☐
- .... ☐
- .... ☐
- .... ☐
- .... ☐
- .... ☐
- .... ☐
- .... ☐

- .... ☐
- .... ☐
- .... ☐
- .... ☐
- .... ☐
- .... ☐
- .... ☐
- .... ☐
- .... ☐

My Winter Hinch List

- .... ☐
- .... ☐
- .... ☐
- .... ☐
- .... ☐
- .... ☐
- .... ☐
- .... ☐
- .... ☐

- .... ☐
- .... ☐
- .... ☐
- .... ☐
- .... ☐
- .... ☐
- .... ☐
- .... ☐

- .... ☐
- .... ☐
- .... ☐
- .... ☐
- .... ☐
- .... ☐
- .... ☐
- .... ☐
- .... ☐

- .... ☐
- .... ☐
- .... ☐
- .... ☐
- .... ☐
- .... ☐
- .... ☐
- .... ☐

TADAA
LISTS

TADAA!

MONDAY

- CLEANED SINK/PLUGS
- MADE BREAKFAST
- TOOK HENRY TO THE PARK
- RADIATOR COVERS
- MADE BEDS
- TIDIED RON'S TOYS AWAY
- WORK EMAILS
- VACUUMED SOFAS

TADAA!

77

TADAA!

TADAA!

TADAA!

TADAA!

-
-
-
-
-
-
-
-

-
-
-
-
-
-
-
-

-
-
-
-
-
-
-

-
-
-
-
-
-
-

TADAA!

_____

_____

- ·····························
- ·····························
- ·····························
- ·····························
- ·····························
- ·····························
- ·····························
- ·····························

- ·····························
- ·····························
- ·····························
- ·····························
- ·····························
- ·····························
- ·····························
- ·····························

_____

_____

- ·····························
- ·····························
- ·····························
- ·····························
- ·····························
- ·····························
- ·····························
- ·····························

- ·····························
- ·····························
- ·····························
- ·····························
- ·····························
- ·····························
- ·····························
- ·····························

82

TADAA!

When a to-do seems a little too much...
Be kind to yourself...

TADAA!

84

TADAA!

TADAA!

TADAA!

TADAA!

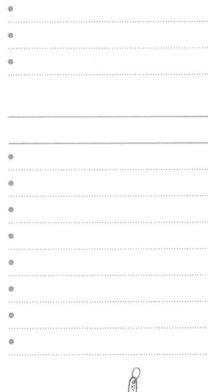

TADAA!

TADAA!

- ....
- ....
- ....
- ....
- ....
- ....
- ....
- ....

- ....
- ....
- ....
- ....
- ....
- ....
- ....

- ....
- ....
- ....
- ....
- ....
- ....
- ....

- ....
- ....
- ....
- ....
- ....
- ....
- ....

TADAA!

You can do anything but not everything.

TADAA!

TADAA!

TADAA!

-
-
-
-
-
-
-

-
-
-
-
-
-

TADAA!

_____

- ....
- ....
- ....
- ....
- ....
- ....
- ....
- ....

_____

- ....
- ....
- ....
- ....
- ....
- ....
- ....
- ....

95

TADAA!

- ....
- ....

- ....
- ....
- ....
- ....
- ....
- ....

	- ....
	- ....
	- ....
	- ....
	- ....
	- ....
	- ....
	- ....

- ....
- ....
- ....
- ....
- ....
- ....
- ....
- ....

TADAA!

-
-
-
-
-
-
-
-

-
-
-
-
-
-
-

TADAA!

TADAA!

Be gentle with yourself...
You're doing the best you can.

FRESH'N UP FRIDAY LISTS

Fresh'n Up Friday

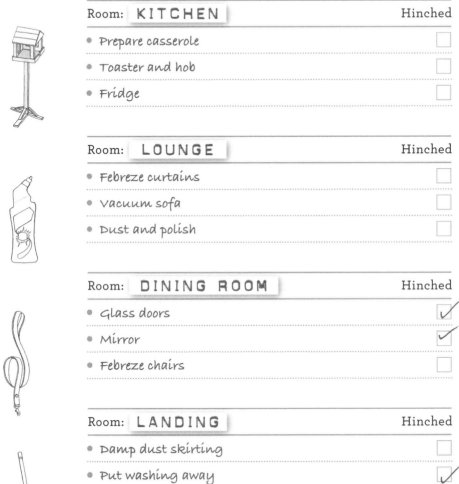

Room: KITCHEN   Hinched

- Prepare casserole ☐
- Toaster and hob ☐
- Fridge ☐

Room: LOUNGE   Hinched

- Febreze curtains ☐
- Vacuum sofa ☐
- Dust and polish ☐

Room: DINING ROOM   Hinched

- Glass doors ☑
- Mirror ☑
- Febreze chairs ☐

Room: LANDING   Hinched

- Damp dust skirting ☐
- Put washing away ☑
- Wipe doors ☑

Fresh'n Up Friday

Room:	Hinched
•	☐
•	☐
•	☐

Room:	Hinched
•	☐
•	☐
•	☐

Room:	Hinched
•	☐
•	☐
•	☐

Room:	Hinched
•	☐
•	☐
•	☐

Fresh'n Up Friday

Room: _____ Hinched

- .... ☐
- .... ☐
- .... ☐

Room: _____ Hinched

- .... ☐
- .... ☐
- .... ☐

Room: _____ Hinched

- .... ☐
- .... ☐
- .... ☐

Room: _____ Hinched

- .... ☐
- .... ☐
- .... ☐

Fresh'n Up Friday

Room: _____ Hinched

- .... ☐
- .... ☐
- .... ☐

Room: _____ Hinched

- .... ☐
- .... ☐
- .... ☐

Room: _____ Hinched

- .... ☐
- .... ☐
- .... ☐

Room: _____ Hinched

- .... ☐
- .... ☐
- .... ☐

Fresh'n Up Friday

Room:	Hinched
•	☐
•	☐
•	☐

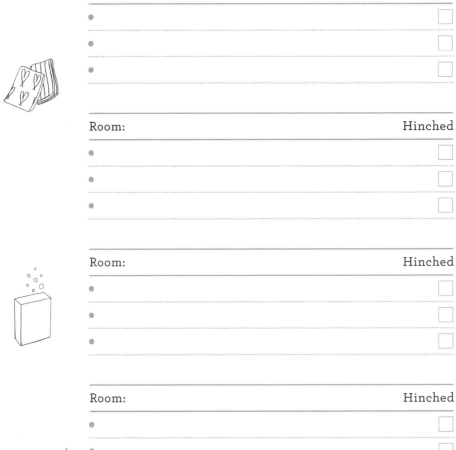

Room:	Hinched
•	☐
•	☐
•	☐

Room:	Hinched
•	☐
•	☐
•	☐

Room:	Hinched
•	☐
•	☐
•	☐

Fresh'n Up Friday

Room: _____ Hinched

- .... ☐
- .... ☐
- .... ☐

Room: _____ Hinched

- .... ☐
- .... ☐
- .... ☐

Room: _____ Hinched

- .... ☐
- .... ☐
- .... ☐

Room: _____ Hinched

- .... ☐
- .... ☐
- .... ☐

Fresh'n Up Friday

Room: .... Hinched

- .... ☐
- .... ☐
- .... ☐

Room: .... Hinched

- .... ☐
- .... ☐
- .... ☐

Room: .... Hinched

- .... ☐
- .... ☐
- .... ☐

Room: .... Hinched

- .... ☐
- .... ☐
- .... ☐

Fresh'n Up Friday

Room: _____ Hinched

- .... ☐
- .... ☐
- .... ☐

Room: _____ Hinched

- .... ☐
- .... ☐
- .... ☐

Room: _____ Hinched

- .... ☐
- .... ☐
- .... ☐

Room: _____ Hinched

- .... ☐
- .... ☐
- .... ☐

Fresh'n Up Friday

Room: _____ Hinched

- .... ☐
- .... ☐
- .... ☐

Room: _____ Hinched

- .... ☐
- .... ☐
- .... ☐

Room: _____ Hinched

- .... ☐
- .... ☐
- .... ☐

Room: _____ Hinched

- .... ☐
- .... ☐
- .... ☐

Fresh'n Up Friday

Room: _____ Hinched

- .... ☐
- .... ☐
- .... ☐

Room: _____ Hinched

- .... ☐
- .... ☐
- .... ☐

Room: _____ Hinched

- .... ☐
- .... ☐
- .... ☐

Room: _____ Hinched

- .... ☐
- .... ☐
- .... ☐

Fresh'n Up Friday

Room: _____ Hinched

- .... ☐
- .... ☐
- .... ☐

Room: _____ Hinched

- .... ☐
- .... ☐
- .... ☐

Room: _____ Hinched

- .... ☐
- .... ☐
- .... ☐

Room: _____ Hinched

- .... ☐
- .... ☐
- .... ☐

Fresh'n Up Friday

Room:	Hinched
•	☐
•	☐
•	☐

Room:	Hinched
•	☐
•	☐
•	☐

Room:	Hinched
•	☐
•	☐
•	☐

Room:	Hinched
•	☐
•	☐
•	☐

Fresh'n Up Friday

Room: .... Hinched

- .... ☐
- .... ☐
- .... ☐

Room: .... Hinched

- .... ☐
- .... ☐
- .... ☐

Room: .... Hinched

- .... ☐
- .... ☐
- .... ☐

Room: .... Hinched

- .... ☐
- .... ☐
- .... ☐

Fresh'n Up Friday

Room: _____ Hinched

- _____ ☐
- _____ ☐
- _____ ☐

Room: _____ Hinched

- _____ ☐
- _____ ☐
- _____ ☐

Room: _____ Hinched

- _____ ☐
- _____ ☐
- _____ ☐

Room: _____ Hinched

- _____ ☐
- _____ ☐
- _____ ☐

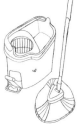

Fresh'n Up Friday

Room: _____ Hinched

- .... ☐
- .... ☐
- .... ☐

Room: _____ Hinched

- .... ☐
- .... ☐
- .... ☐

Room: _____ Hinched

- .... ☐
- .... ☐
- .... ☐

Room: _____ Hinched

- .... ☐
- .... ☐
- .... ☐

Fresh'n Up Friday

Room: _____ Hinched

- ⬤ _____ ☐
- ⬤ _____ ☐
- ⬤ _____ ☐

Room: _____ Hinched

- ⬤ _____ ☐
- ⬤ _____ ☐
- ⬤ _____ ☐

Room: _____ Hinched

- ⬤ _____ ☐
- ⬤ _____ ☐
- ⬤ _____ ☐

Room: _____ Hinched

- ⬤ _____ ☐
- ⬤ _____ ☐
- ⬤ _____ ☐

Fresh'n Up Friday

Room:	Hinched
•	☐
•	☐
•	☐

Room:	Hinched
•	☐
•	☐
•	☐

Room:	Hinched
•	☐
•	☐
•	☐

Room:	Hinched
•	☐
•	☐
•	☐

Fresh'n Up Friday

Room: _____ Hinched

- .... ☐
- .... ☐
- .... ☐

Room: _____ Hinched

- .... ☐
- .... ☐
- .... ☐

Room: _____ Hinched

- .... ☐
- .... ☐
- .... ☐

Room: _____ Hinched

- .... ☐
- .... ☐
- .... ☐

ME TIME LISTS

You'll be amazed at what you
attract when you start believing
in what you deserve.

You don't have to be perfect.
Having a bad day is okay and
asking for help is strength.

Never forget you have a special
magic about you that is uniquely yours.
Please always remember to take
the best care of yourself.

I'd love you to use these pages
to make a promise to do something
just for you, every day.

Weekly Me Time

Use these pages to plan out your weekly self-care.

Monday

- Take Henry to the field ✓
- Garden centre with Mum ✓
- Calm app before bed ✓

Tuesday

- Plant seeds ✓
- Organise photo albums ✓
- Practise Spanish ✓

Wednesday

- Phone in the drawer day ✓
- Lunch from the caf ✓
- Try new recipe for dinner ✓

Thursday

- Apply self tanner ✓
- Hair mask ✓
- Face mask ✓

Friday

- Take Len out in the stroller ✓
- Get ready to go out ✓
- Dinner with my best friends ✓

Saturday

- Have a lie-in ✓
- Drive in countryside ✓
- Get takeaway ✓

Sunday

- Ron & Mummy – soft play ☐
- Family walk to The Prom ☐
- After-dinner ice cream trip ☐
- Write out new affirmations ☐
- Write out my Hinch List ☐

A typical example of my weekly Me Time promise!

Me Time Ideas

Use these examples as inspiration for when you are finding it tricky to think of self-care ideas.

Walk a fur baby

Learn a new skill

Take a nap

Start a new hobby / practise an old one

Try a new recipe

Digital cleanse

Journal

Sleep in

Enjoy your favourite meal

Enjoy a pedicure

Yoga

Have a no phone day / set amount of time

Dance and sing like no one's watching!

Buy yourself a gift or flowers

Spa day

Plan a holiday

Do nothing at all

Go for a walk

Take your time
getting ready

Write a gratitude list

Have a relaxing bath

Spend time with
your little family

Listen to a podcast
or music

Read a book /
listen to an audiobook

Apply a face /
hair mask

Organise /
declutter an area

Go to bed early

Meditate /
breathing exercises

Paint your nails

Watch a movie

Cuddle a fur baby

Scrapbook /
organise photos

Exercise

Date: ....

Weekly Me Time

Use these pages to plan out your weekly self-care.

Monday

- .... ☐
- .... ☐
- .... ☐

Tuesday

- .... ☐
- .... ☐
- .... ☐

Wednesday

- .... ☐
- .... ☐
- .... ☐

Thursday

- .... ☐
- .... ☐
- .... ☐

Friday

- .... ☐
- .... ☐
- .... ☐

Saturday

- .... ☐
- .... ☐
- .... ☐

Sunday

- .... ☐
- .... ☐
- .... ☐
- .... ☐
- .... ☐

Weekly Me Time

Use these pages to plan out your weekly self-care.

Monday

- ☐
- ☐
- ☐

Tuesday

- ☐
- ☐
- ☐

Wednesday

- ☐
- ☐
- ☐

Thursday

- ☐
- ☐
- ☐

Date: ....

Friday

- ☐
- ☐
- ☐

Saturday

- ☐
- ☐
- ☐

Sunday

- ☐
- ☐
- ☐
- ☐
- ☐

You are perfect just as you are.

Weekly Me Time

Use these pages to plan out your weekly self-care.

Monday

- ♡ .... ☐
- ♡ .... ☐
- ♡ .... ☐

Friday

- ♡ .... ☐
- ♡ .... ☐
- ♡ .... ☐

Tuesday

- ♡ .... ☐
- ♡ .... ☐
- ♡ .... ☐

Saturday

- ♡ .... ☐
- ♡ .... ☐
- ♡ .... ☐

Wednesday

- ♡ .... ☐
- ♡ .... ☐
- ♡ .... ☐

Sunday

- ♡ .... ☐
- ♡ .... ☐
- ♡ .... ☐
- ♡ .... ☐
- ♡ .... ☐

Thursday

- ♡ .... ☐
- ♡ .... ☐
- ♡ .... ☐

Weekly Me Time

Use these pages to plan out your weekly self-care.

Monday

- ♡ .... ☐
- ♡ .... ☐
- ♡ .... ☐

Tuesday

- ♡ .... ☐
- ♡ .... ☐
- ♡ .... ☐

Wednesday

- ♡ .... ☐
- ♡ .... ☐
- ♡ .... ☐

Thursday

- ♡ .... ☐
- ♡ .... ☐
- ♡ .... ☐

Friday

- ♡ .... ☐
- ♡ .... ☐
- ♡ .... ☐

Saturday

- ♡ .... ☐
- ♡ .... ☐
- ♡ .... ☐

Sunday

- ♡ .... ☐
- ♡ .... ☐
- ♡ .... ☐
- ♡ .... ☐
- ♡ .... ☐

Date: ....

Weekly Me Time

Use these pages to plan out your weekly self-care.

Monday

- .... ☐
- .... ☐
- .... ☐

Tuesday

- .... ☐
- .... ☐
- .... ☐

Wednesday

- .... ☐
- .... ☐
- .... ☐

Thursday

- .... ☐
- .... ☐
- .... ☐

Friday

- .... ☐
- .... ☐
- .... ☐

Saturday

- .... ☐
- .... ☐
- .... ☐

Sunday

- .... ☐
- .... ☐
- .... ☐
- .... ☐
- .... ☐

Taking care of yourself is a necessity, not a luxury.

130

Weekly Me Time

Use these pages to plan out your weekly self-care.

Monday

- .... ☐
- .... ☐
- .... ☐

Tuesday

- .... ☐
- .... ☐
- .... ☐

Wednesday

- .... ☐
- .... ☐
- .... ☐

Thursday

- .... ☐
- .... ☐
- .... ☐

Friday

- .... ☐
- .... ☐
- .... ☐

Saturday

- .... ☐
- .... ☐
- .... ☐

Sunday

- .... ☐
- .... ☐
- .... ☐
- .... ☐
- .... ☐

Date: ....

Weekly Me Time

Use these pages to plan out your weekly self-care.

Monday

☆ _____ ☐

☆ _____ ☐

☆ _____ ☐

Tuesday

☆ _____ ☐

☆ _____ ☐

☆ _____ ☐

Wednesday

☆ _____ ☐

☆ _____ ☐

☆ _____ ☐

Thursday

☆ _____ ☐

☆ _____ ☐

☆ _____ ☐

Friday

☆ _____ ☐

☆ _____ ☐

☆ _____ ☐

Saturday

☆ _____ ☐

☆ _____ ☐

☆ _____ ☐

Sunday

☆ _____ ☐

☆ _____ ☐

☆ _____ ☐

☆ _____ ☐

☆ _____ ☐

Weekly Me Time

Use these pages to plan out your weekly self-care.

Monday

☆ .... ☐
☆ .... ☐
☆ .... ☐

Tuesday

☆ .... ☐
☆ .... ☐
☆ .... ☐

Wednesday

☆ .... ☐
☆ .... ☐
☆ .... ☐

Thursday

☆ .... ☐
☆ .... ☐
☆ .... ☐

Friday

☆ .... ☐
☆ .... ☐
☆ .... ☐

Saturday

☆ .... ☐
☆ .... ☐
☆ .... ☐

Sunday

☆ .... ☐
☆ .... ☐
☆ .... ☐
☆ .... ☐
☆ .... ☐

Weekly Me Time

Use these pages to plan out your weekly self-care.

Monday

- [ ] ....
- [ ] ....
- [ ] ....

Friday

- [ ] ....
- [ ] ....
- [ ] ....

Tuesday

- [ ] ....
- [ ] ....
- [ ] ....

Saturday

- [ ] ....
- [ ] ....
- [ ] ....

Wednesday

- [ ] ....
- [ ] ....
- [ ] ....

Sunday

- [ ] ....
- [ ] ....
- [ ] ....
- [ ] ....

Thursday

- [ ] ....
- [ ] ....
- [ ] ....

Date: ....

Weekly Me Time

Use these pages to plan out your weekly self-care.

Monday

- ☐
- ☐
- ☐

Tuesday

- ☐
- ☐
- ☐

Wednesday

- ☐
- ☐
- ☐

Thursday

- ☐
- ☐
- ☐

Friday

- ☐
- ☐
- ☐

Saturday

- ☐
- ☐

Sunday

- ☐
- ☐
- ☐
- ☐
- ☐

When you say 'yes' to others, make sure you aren't saying 'no' to yourself.

Date: ....

Weekly Me Time

Use these pages to plan out your weekly self-care.

Monday
♡ .... ☐
♡ .... ☐
♡ .... ☐

Tuesday
♡ .... ☐
♡ .... ☐
♡ .... ☐

Wednesday
♡ .... ☐
♡ .... ☐
♡ .... ☐

Thursday
♡ .... ☐
♡ .... ☐
♡ .... ☐

Friday
♡ .... ☐
♡ .... ☐
♡ .... ☐

Saturday
♡ .... ☐
♡ .... ☐
♡ .... ☐

Sunday
♡ .... ☐
♡ .... ☐
♡ .... ☐
♡ .... ☐

Weekly Me Time

Use these pages to plan out your weekly self-care.

Monday

♡ .... ☐
♡ .... ☐
♡ .... ☐

Tuesday

♡ .... ☐
♡ .... ☐
♡ .... ☐

Wednesday

♡ .... ☐
♡ .... ☐
♡ .... ☐

Thursday

♡ .... ☐
♡ .... ☐
♡ .... ☐

Friday

♡ .... ☐
♡ .... ☐
♡ .... ☐

Saturday

♡ .... ☐
♡ .... ☐
♡ .... ☐

Sunday

♡ .... ☐
♡ .... ☐
♡ .... ☐
♡ .... ☐
♡ .... ☐

Date: ....

Weekly Me Time

Use these pages to plan out your weekly self-care.

Monday

- .... ☐
- .... ☐
- .... ☐

Tuesday

- .... ☐
- .... ☐
- .... ☐

Wednesday

- .... ☐
- .... ☐
- .... ☐

Thursday

- .... ☐
- .... ☐
- .... ☐

Friday

- .... ☐
- .... ☐
- .... ☐

Saturday

- .... ☐
- .... ☐
- .... ☐

Sunday

- .... ☐
- .... ☐
- .... ☐
- .... ☐
- .... ☐

Your best is enough.

Weekly Me Time

Use these pages to plan out your weekly self-care.

Monday

- ▢
- ▢
- ▢

Tuesday

- ▢
- ▢
- ▢

Wednesday

- ▢
- ▢
- ▢

Thursday

- ▢
- ▢
- ▢

Friday

- ▢
- ▢
- ▢

Saturday

- ▢
- ▢
- ▢

Sunday

- ▢
- ▢
- ▢
- ▢
- ▢

Date: ....

Weekly Me Time

Use these pages to plan out your weekly self-care.

Monday

☆ .... ☐
☆ .... ☐
☆ .... ☐

Tuesday

☆ .... ☐
☆ .... ☐
☆ .... ☐

Wednesday

☆ .... ☐
☆ .... ☐
☆ .... ☐

Thursday

☆ .... ☐
☆ .... ☐
☆ .... ☐

Friday

☆ .... ☐
☆ .... ☐
☆ .... ☐

Saturday

☆ .... ☐
☆ .... ☐
☆ .... ☐

Sunday

☆ .... ☐
☆ .... ☐
☆ .... ☐
☆ .... ☐
☆ .... ☐

Weekly Me Time

Use these pages to plan out your weekly self-care.

Monday
☆ .... ☐
☆ .... ☐
☆ .... ☐

Tuesday
☆ .... ☐
☆ .... ☐
☆ .... ☐

Wednesday
☆ .... ☐
☆ .... ☐
☆ .... ☐

Thursday
☆ .... ☐
☆ .... ☐
☆ .... ☐

Friday
☆ .... ☐
☆ .... ☐
☆ .... ☐

Saturday
☆ .... ☐
☆ .... ☐
☆ .... ☐

Sunday
☆ .... ☐
☆ .... ☐
☆ .... ☐
☆ .... ☐
☆ .... ☐

GRATITUDE
LISTS

Date: *Monday 10th*

This Week I Am Grateful For...

Write down three things that made each of your days brighter.

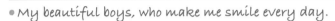

Monday

- My beautiful boys, who make me smile every day.
- The amazing sunshine today – it's finally starting to feel like spring!
- Ben & Jerry's Caramel Chew Chew. Nothing else quite hits the spot!

Tuesday

- I had less of a nervous tummy today than usual and it felt amazing.
- Interesting product launch call. I love learning all about the science!
- My little work team who have become like family.

Wednesday

- Mum and Dad – having them close and around so much is such a blessing.
- The amazing work opportunity I was offered.
- Shining my sink! I know my Hinchers will understand the satisfaction!

Thursday

- My lovely followers who were there to talk to when I wasn't feeling my best.
- Being able to hug my family.
- Sitting in the boys' rooms tidying through their stuff.

Friday

- Having Jamie at home to support me. Couldn't do this without him!
- My homeware range – to see my pieces in your homes gives me butterflies.
- Going to the hairdresser. Feels amazing to feel more like myself again.

Saturday

- Lunch at The Prom with my friend and our little ones.
- My sister Sam. My best friend for life who will always have my back.
- Both Ron & Len were asleep by bedtime so Jamie and I managed to watch a movie!

Sunday

- A lie-in – I feel brand new!
- Our family picnic at Henry's favourite field.
- My best friends – who are always at the end of the phone when I need someone to talk to.

A typical example of my Gratitude List!

Date: ....

This Week I Am Grateful For...

Write down three things that made each of your days brighter.

Monday

♡ ....
....

♡ ....
....

♡ ....
....

Tuesday

♡ ....
....

♡ ....
....

♡ ....
....

Friday

♡ ....
....

♡ ....
....

♡ ....
....

Saturday

♡ ....
....

♡ ....
....

♡ ....
....

Wednesday

♡ ....
....
♡ ....
....
♡ ....
....
....

Thursday

♡ ....
....
♡ ....
....
♡ ....
....

Sunday

♡ ....
....
♡ ....
....
♡ ....
....

The more you practise being thankful for your life, the more you'll see everything there is to be thankful for.

♡

Date: ....

This Week I Am Grateful For...

Write down three things that made each of your days brighter.

Monday

- ....
- ....
- ....

Tuesday

- ....
- ....
- ....

Wednesday

- ....
- ....
- ....

Thursday

- ....
- ....
- ....

Friday

-
-
-

Saturday

-
-
-

Sunday

-
-
-

Date: ....

This Week I Am Grateful For...

Write down three things that made each of your days brighter.

Monday

☆ ....
....

☆ ....
....
....

☆ ....
....
....

Tuesday

☆ ....
....

☆ ....
....
....

☆ ....
....
....

Friday

☆ ....
....

☆ ....
....
....

☆ ....
....
....

Saturday

☆ ....
....

☆ ....
....
....

☆ ....
....
....

Wednesday

☆
....
....
☆
....
....
☆
....
....

Thursday

☆
....
....
☆
....
....
☆
....
....

Sunday

☆
....
....
☆
....
....
☆
....
....

Date: ....

This Week I Am Grateful For...

Write down three things that made each of your days brighter.

Monday

- ....
- ....
- ....

Tuesday

- ....
- ....
- ....

Wednesday

- ....
- ....
- ....

Thursday

- ....
- ....
- ....

Friday

-
-
-

Saturday

-
-
-

Sunday

-
-
-

It's so important to find the good in each and every day. No matter how big or how small, you'll soon realise there are so many things in life to be thankful for.

153

Date: ....

This Week I Am Grateful For ...

Write down three things that made each of your days brighter.

Monday
♡ ....
....
♡ ....
....
♡ ....
....
....

Tuesday
♡ ....
....
♡ ....
....
♡ ....
....
....

Friday
♡ ....
....
♡ ....
....
♡ ....
....
....

Saturday
♡ ....
....
♡ ....
....
♡ ....
....
....

Wednesday

♡ ....
....
♡ ....
....
♡ ....
....

Thursday

♡ ....
....
♡ ....
....
♡ ....
....

Sunday

♡ ....
....
♡ ....
....
♡ ....
....

Date: ....

This Week I Am Grateful For...

Write down three things that made each of your days brighter.

Monday
- ....
- ....
- ....

Tuesday
- ....
- ....
- ....

Wednesday
- ....
- ....
- ....

Thursday
- ....
- ....
- ....

Friday

- ....
- ....
- ....

Saturday

- ....
- ....
- ....

Sunday

- ....
- ....
- ....

Date: ....

This Week I Am Grateful For...

Write down three things that made each of your days brighter.

Monday
☆
☆
☆

Tuesday
☆
☆
☆

Friday
☆
☆
☆

Saturday
☆
☆
☆

Wednesday

⭐ ....
....
⭐ ....
....
⭐ ....
....

Thursday

⭐ ....
....
⭐ ....
....
⭐ ....
....

Sunday

⭐ ....
....
⭐ ....
....
⭐ ....
....

In case no one has reminded you today: You are beautiful. You are loved. You are strong. You are needed. You are enough.

♡

Date: ....

This Week I Am Grateful For...

Write down three things that made each of your days brighter.

Monday

- ....
- ....
- ....

Tuesday

- ....
- ....
- ....

Wednesday

- ....
- ....
- ....

Thursday

- ....
- ....
- ....

Friday

-
-
-

Saturday

-
-
-

Sunday

-
-
-

Date: ....

This Week I Am Grateful For...

Write down three things that made each of your days brighter.

Monday

♡ ....

....

♡ ....

....

♡ ....

....

Tuesday

♡ ....

....

♡ ....

....

♡ ....

....

Friday

♡ ....

....

♡ ....

....

♡ ....

....

Saturday

♡ ....

....

♡ ....

....

♡ ....

....

Wednesday

♡ ....

....

♡ ....

....

♡ ....

....

Thursday

♡ ....

....

♡ ....

....

♡ ....

....

Sunday

♡ ....

....

♡ ....

....

♡ ....

....

Date: ....

This Week I Am Grateful For...

Write down three things that made each of your days brighter.

Monday

- ....
- ....
- ....

Tuesday

- ....
- ....
- ....

Wednesday

- ....
- ....
- ....

Thursday

- ....
- ....
- ....

Friday

-
-
-

Saturday

-
-
-

Sunday

-
-
-

*What is meant for you will
never pass you by.*

Date: ....

This Week I Am Grateful For...

Write down three things that made each of your days brighter.

Monday

☆ ....
....
....

☆ ....
....
....

☆ ....
....
....

Tuesday

☆ ....
....
....

☆ ....
....
....

☆ ....
....
....

Friday

☆ ....
....
....

☆ ....
....
....

☆ ....
....
....

Saturday

☆ ....
....
....

☆ ....
....
....

☆ ....
....
....

WASH UP

Wednesday

☆ ....
....
☆ ....
....
☆ ....
....

Thursday

☆ ....
....
☆ ....
....
☆ ....
....

Sunday

☆ ....
....
☆ ....
....
☆ ....
....

This Week I Am Grateful For...

Write down three things that made each of your days brighter.

Monday

- ....
- ....
- ....

Tuesday

- ....
- ....
- ....

Wednesday

- ....
- ....
- ....

Thursday

- ....
- ....
- ....

Friday

-
-
-

Saturday

-
-
-

Sunday

-
-
-

Date: ....

This Week I Am Grateful For...

Write down three things that made each of your days brighter.

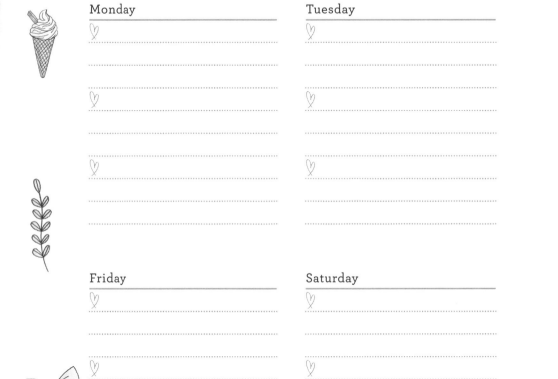

Monday
♡
....
....
♡
....
....
♡
....
....

Tuesday
♡
....
....
♡
....
....
♡
....
....

Friday
♡
....
....
♡
....
....
♡
....
....

Saturday
♡
....
....
♡
....
....
♡
....
....

Wednesday

Thursday

Sunday

Being grateful turns what we already have into enough.

Date: ....

This Week I Am Grateful For...

Write down three things that made each of your days brighter.

Monday
- ....
- ....
- ....

Tuesday
- ....
- ....
- ....

Wednesday
- ....
- ....
- ....

Thursday
- ....
- ....
- ....

Friday

-
-
-

Saturday

-
-
-

Sunday

-
-
-

Date: ....

This Week I Am Grateful For...

Write down three things that made each of your days brighter.

Monday
☆ ....
....
....
☆ ....
....
....
☆ ....
....
....

Tuesday
☆ ....
....
....
☆ ....
....
....
☆ ....
....
....

Friday
☆ ....
....
....
☆ ....
....
....
☆ ....
....
....

Saturday
☆ ....
....
....
☆ ....
....
....
☆ ....
....
....

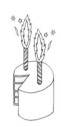

Wednesday

☆ ....
....
....
☆ ....
....
....
☆ ....
....
....

Thursday

☆ ....
....
....
☆ ....
....
....
☆ ....
....
....

Sunday

☆ ....
....
....
☆ ....
....
....
☆ ....
....
....

Date: ....

This Week I Am Grateful For...

Write down three things that made each of your days brighter.

Monday

- ....
- ....
- ....

Tuesday

- ....
- ....
- ....

Wednesday

- ....
- ....
- ....

Thursday

- ....
- ....
- ....

Friday

-
-
-

Saturday

-
-
-

Sunday

-
-
-

Appreciate the little things, because one day you'll look back and realise they were the big things.

MAKE YOUR
DREAMS
COME
TRUE

Here are some of my dreams!

The Big Picture

Use this page to write down all your life dreams.
The things you believe will make you truly happy. It doesn't
matter how big or little they seem.

My Dreams:

☆ Learn Spanish
☆ Go on safari
☆ Improve my cooking
☆ Hinch Farm
☆ Expand my homeware range
☆ Utility room
☆ Sing in a studio
☆ Stay in a log cabin
☆ Go to Lapland
☆
☆
☆

☆
☆
☆
☆
☆
☆
☆
☆
☆
☆
☆

Choose the dreams you'd like to turn into goals.
Use the mind maps to organise your initial
thoughts and then create a plan of action
using the goal planning pages.

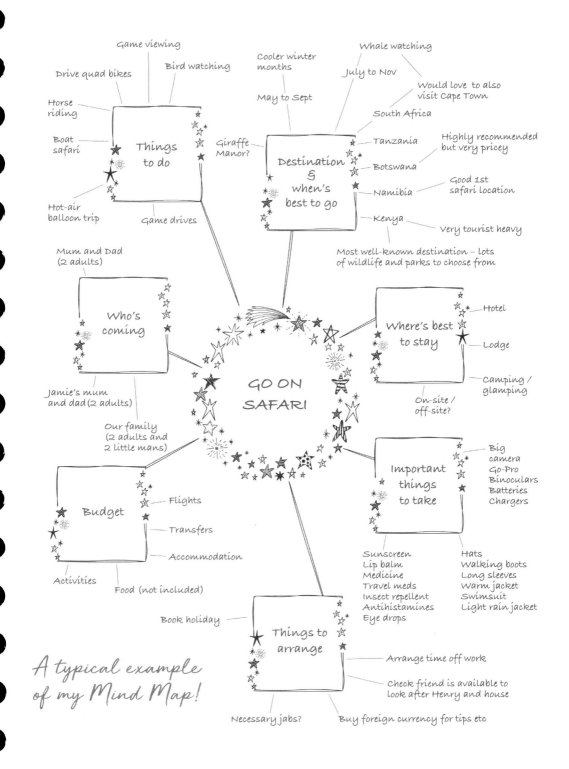

Game viewing

Drive quad bikes

Bird watching

Horse riding

Boat safari

Things to do

Hot-air balloon trip

Game drives

Giraffe Manor?

Cooler winter months

May to Sept

Whale watching

July to Nov

Would love to also visit Cape Town

South Africa

Destination & when's best to go

Tanzania — Highly recommended but very pricey

Botswana

Namibia — Good 1st safari location

Kenya — Very tourist heavy

Most well-known destination – lots of wildlife and parks to choose from

Mum and Dad (2 adults)

Who's coming

Jamie's mum and dad (2 adults)

Our family (2 adults and 2 little mans)

GO ON SAFARI

Where's best to stay

Hotel

Lodge

Camping / glamping

On-site / off-site?

Important things to take

Big camera
Go-Pro
Binoculars
Batteries
Chargers

Sunscreen
Lip balm
Medicine
Travel meds
Insect repellent
Antihistamines
Eye drops

Hats
Walking boots
Long sleeves
Warm jacket
Swimsuit
Light rain jacket

Budget

Flights

Transfers

Accommodation

Activities

Food (not included)

Book holiday

Things to arrange

Arrange time off work

Check friend is available to look after Henry and house

Buy foreign currency for tips etc

Necessary jabs?

A typical example of my Mind Map!

Goal

GO ON SAFARI!

Date created: _10th May_   Achieve by: _aim for Sep 2023_

Why is this goal important to me?

Wanted to go on safari for as long as I can remember. It would be absolutely amazing to take the boys and for them to experience these incredible animals in their natural habitat. Unforgettable family memories to be made. Never been on a big holiday like this, both sides together. Would be such a special time!

What do I need to achieve my goal?

- Research – internet, travel agency, brochures, speak to friends
- Time – time off to go, set aside to research & plan everything
- Family – get together to discuss availability, where to go & activities
- Cost – set up a budget plan spreadsheet. Work out the cost for everything required

A typical example of my Goal Plan!

How am I going to achieve my goal?

* Research – set aside time to research destinations. Use mind maps to list pros & cons. Present to family. Set up spreadsheet for financy bits.   Achieve by: Jun 2022

* Budget – travel, accommodation, food, activities, spending money etc. Plan using budget spreadsheet. Check in & review periodically.   Achieve by: Jun 2022

* Book – organise Henry & house sitter. Book leave, book holiday (decide whether to use agency or DIY), sort jabs, insurance, currency, passports etc.   Achieve by: Sep 2022

* Plan – write out lists of what we need to take & then split between stuff we already have & stuff we need to get. Slowly start to pick up items & store safely.   Achieve by: Dec 2022

* Closer to the time – how to get to the airport – all together/ different cars? Book stay in long-stay carpark? Hotel? Hire car the other end? Layover?   Achieve by: May 2023

How will I feel achieving my goal? What will my reward be?

Absolutely indescribable. Once in a lifetime holiday. Memories made & quality family time – priceless!

Completed

The Big Picture

Use this page to write down all your life dreams.
The things you believe will make you truly happy. It doesn't
matter how big or little they seem.

My Dreams

Now it's your turn!
Once you've used the space above to decide what
will make you truly happy, choose the dreams you'd
like to turn into goals and use the mind maps and
goal planning pages to make them happen!

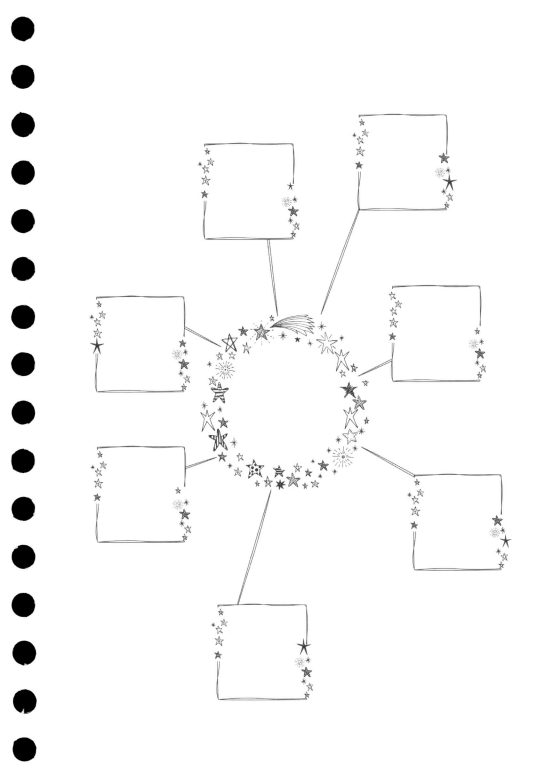

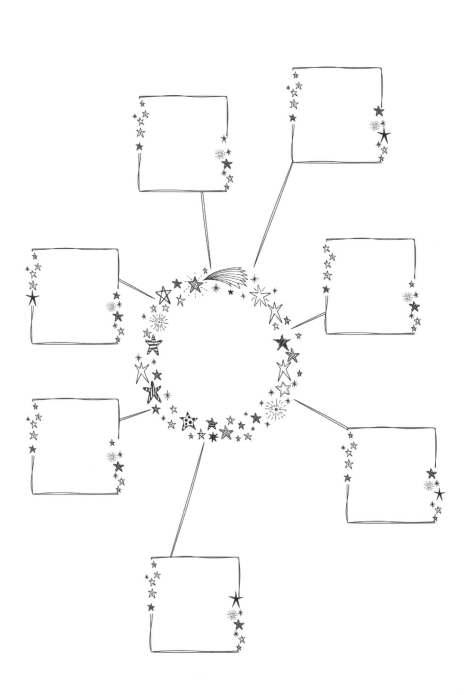

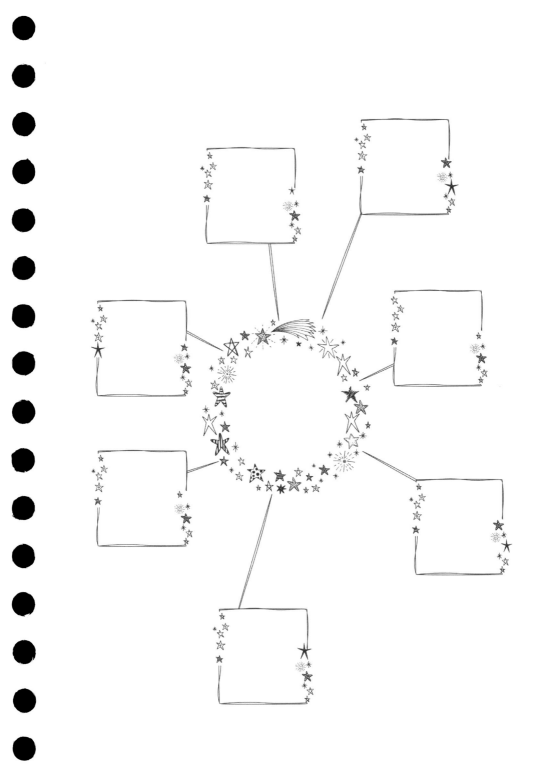

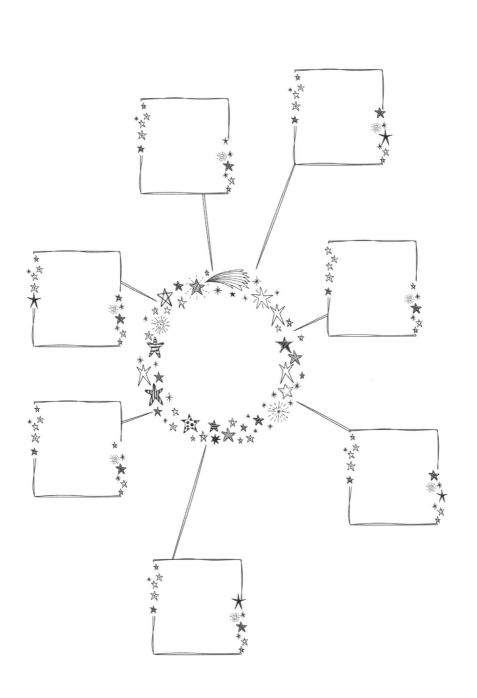

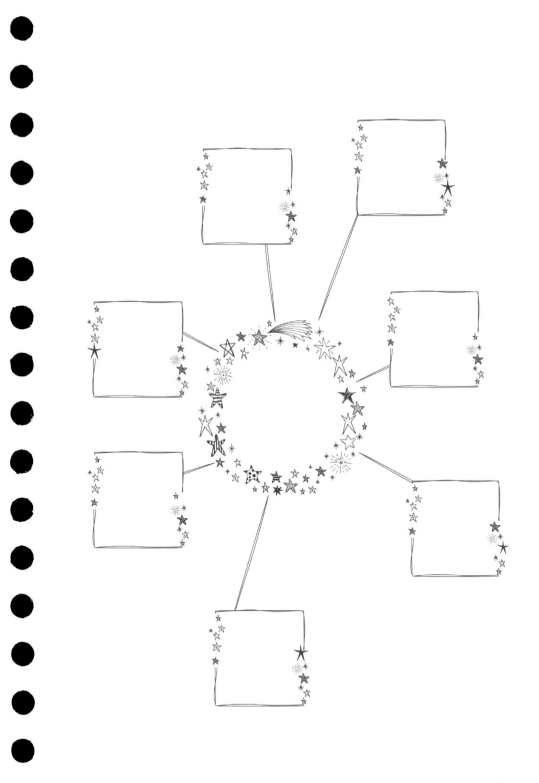

Goal

Date created: ....   Achieve by: ....

Why is this goal important to me?

....

....

....

....

....

What do I need to achieve my goal?

- ....
- ....
- ....
- ....
- ....

Goals are simply your dreams, but with a plan.

How am I going to achieve my goal?

- ....
  ....
  ....   Achieve by: .... ☆

- ....
  ....
  ....   Achieve by: .... ☆

- ....
  ....
  ....   Achieve by: .... ☆

- ....
  ....
  ....   Achieve by: .... ☆

- ....
  ....
  ....   Achieve by: .... ☆

How will I feel achieving my goal? What will my reward be?

....

....

Completed

Goal

....

Date created: .... Achieve by: ....

Why is this goal important to me?

....

....

....

....

....

What do I need to achieve my goal?

- ....
- ....
- ....
- ....
- ....

How am I going to achieve my goal?

- ....

....

.... Achieve by: .... ☆

- ....

....

.... Achieve by: .... ☆

- ....

....

.... Achieve by: .... ☆

- ....

....

.... Achieve by: .... ☆

- ....

....

.... Achieve by: .... ☆

How will I feel achieving my goal? What will my reward be?

....

....

Completed

Goal

Date created: .... Achieve by: ....

Why is this goal important to me?

....

....

....

....

....

What do I need to achieve my goal?

- ....

- ....

- ....

- ....

- ....

*The sooner you start believing in yourself,
the sooner you'll start to see results.*

How am I going to achieve my goal?

- ....

  ....

  .... Achieve by: .... ☆
- ....

  ....

  .... Achieve by: .... ☆
- ....

  ....

  .... Achieve by: .... ☆
- ....

  ....

  .... Achieve by: .... ☆
- ....

  ....

  .... Achieve by: .... ☆

How will I feel achieving my goal? What will my reward be?

....

....

Completed

Goal

....

Date created: .... Achieve by: ....

Why is this goal important to me?

....

....

....

....

....

What do I need to achieve my goal?

- ....
- ....
- ....
- ....
- ....

How am I going to achieve my goal?

- ....

....
Achieve by: .... ☆

- ....

....
Achieve by: .... ☆

- ....

....
Achieve by: .... ☆

- ....

....
Achieve by: .... ☆

- ....

....
Achieve by: .... ☆

How will I feel achieving my goal? What will my reward be?

....

....

 Completed

Goal

Date created: ....   Achieve by: ....

Why is this goal important to me?

....

....

....

....

....

What do I need to achieve my goal?

- ....

- ....

- ....

- ....

- ....

Grateful for where I am . . .
Excited for what's still to come.

How am I going to achieve my goal?

- ....
....

                                              Achieve by: .... ☆
- ....

                                              Achieve by: .... ☆
- ....

                                              Achieve by: .... ☆
- ....

                                              Achieve by: .... ☆
- ....

                                              Achieve by: .... ☆

How will I feel achieving my goal? What will my reward be?

....

....

Completed

NOTES
AND
LISTS

Because we all work in our own unique ways, here are some more pages to organise your days.

Here are some examples of what I will be using these pages for:

* Important dates to remember
* Meal plans
* Birthdays
* Appointments
* Holiday planning
* Shopping lists
* Work to do
* Emails to action
* Content posting ideas

- .... ☐   - .... ☐
- .... ☐   - .... ☐
- .... ☐   - .... ☐
- .... ☐   - .... ☐
- .... ☐   - .... ☐
- .... ☐   - .... ☐
- .... ☐   - .... ☐
- .... ☐   - .... ☐
- .... ☐   - .... ☐
- .... ☐   - .... ☐
- .... ☐   - .... ☐
- .... ☐   - .... ☐
- .... ☐   - .... ☐
- .... ☐   - .... ☐
- .... ☐   - .... ☐
- .... ☐   - .... ☐
- .... ☐   - .... ☐
- .... ☐   - .... ☐
- .... ☐   - .... ☐

206

210

212

214

You Did It!
All The Best
xx